Eimhir

Somhairle MacGill-Eain

'Lànachd an eòlais m' an cùrsa,
failmhe an aineolais gun iùl-chairt,
cruinne-cè a' gluasad sàmhach
aigne leatha fhèin san àrainn'

Eimhir

Somhairle MacGill-Eain

acair

Chaidh *Dàin do Eimhir* fhoillseachadh an toiseach ann an 1943
le Uilleam MacGIllFhaolain, an Glaschu.

Chaidh *Poems to Eimhir* fhoillseachadh an toiseach ann an 1971
le Northern House, Newcastle on Tyne.

An leabhar seo foillsichte an 1999, le Acair Earranta,
7 Sràid Sheumais, Steòrnabhagh, Eilean Leòdhais.

Clò-bhuailte le ColourBooks, Bail' Ath Cliath

Chuidich Comhairle nan Leabhraichean am foillsichear
le cosgaisean an leabhair seo.

Tha Acair a' toirt taing do Chomunn Gàidhlig Inbhir Nis airson
an co-obrachaidh, am misneachaidh agus an taic airgid.

Tha Acair cuideachd a' toirt taing do Renee NicGill-Eain
agus do Dhonalda Nic A' Ghobhainn airson cead a thoirt
don leabhar seo a dhol air adhart.

LAGE/ISBN 0 86152 201 X (Hb)
LAGE/ISBN 0 86152 295 8 (Pb)

Clàr-innse / Contents

FOREWORD

THE POET AND THE TRANSLATOR:
AN APPRECIATION

This book has an important place in the history of modern Gaelic literature, as it has been produced by a convergence of the poetic skills of two of Scotland's best known twentieth-century poets, both of them Gaelic-speaking islanders - Sorley MacLean and Iain Crichton Smith. Sadly, they are no longer with us. Sorley MacLean died in November 1996, and Iain Crichton Smith in October 1998. We mourn their recent passing, and for that reason this record of their creative interaction as poets is especially poignant. As a tribute to the two poets and their achievements, it is now republished by Acair in conjunction with the Gaelic Society of Inverness. Sorley MacLean was Bard to the Society from 1945 until his death, and read most of his major critical papers to meetings of the Society. Iain Crichton Smith was a Life Member.

Curiously, I have a vivid recollection of the period when Iain Crichton Smith was engaged in translating the poetry of Sorley MacLean. I was a pupil in Oban High School at that time, and, in the early summer of 1967, I was given (not for the first time!) a flimsy cardboard box containing recent writing by 'Mr Smith'. I was duly instructed to keep it 'over the weekend' and tell him what I thought of its contents. As the result of earlier conversations, 'Mr Smith' - an inspirational teacher of English - was anxious to share his insights into the poetry of Sorley MacLean with a young pupil who was making his first attempt to understand a little of what Sorley MacLean had captured in breathtakingly new Gaelic verse. I can still see vividly the almost transparent sheets of copy-paper which had endured the remorseless onslaught of Iain's typewriter, as it blasted its way through blue carbon. Iain used his typewriter like a cannon, firing letters at all parts of the page. I read the translations, and was impressed (even then) by their fidelity to the originals, and by the way in which Iain Crichton Smith had reproduced the nuances of Sorley MacLean's thought, sometimes adhering very closely to the original Gaelic versions, but also (at times) gently remoulding and supplementing the text to emphasise particular meanings. It was very evident that the one poet was responding to the other in a deep exchange of insights. Typically, Iain Smith was utterly self-effacing about his translations, and they did not appear in print until 1971; his concern was not to produce another book, but to communicate the essence of the poet whose voice had so captivated his own mind. He admired MacLean's poetry too deeply to publish his translations quickly; it was a source of encouragement and inspiration to him. So too was the man himself. Sometimes Iain would let slip that Sorley was coming to Oban, and that he would be meeting him. Sorley would be visiting his brother, John, the incomparable and (by 1967) recently retired Rector of Oban High School, whose profound Classical scholarship was complemented by a radiantly warm Gaelic humanity.

The intellectual bond between the two poets was strong. Iain Crichton Smith was constantly aware of the 'revolutionary' nature of Sorley MacLean's verse. As he says in his introduction to the translations, he found it 'little short of miraculous' that such a remarkable 'union of the sophisticated and the primitive, of the intelligence and the passions', should have emerged from the Gaelic world in the 1930s. In retrospect, twenty-five years and more since Iain Crichton Smith wrote the introduction to this book, what is no less remarkable is the manner in which the creation of high-quality, modern Gaelic verse has been maintained within the Gaelic world. In sustaining this ongoing 'union of the sophisticated and the primitive, of the intelligence and the passions' beyond the foundational contribution of Sorley MacLean, nobody was more influential, nobody more of a 'revolutionary', than Iain Crichton Smith himself.

This book testifies to a highly creative union of minds between Sorley MacLean and Iain Crichton Smith. I remember well how, on one occasion, Iain talked informally to a number of pupils about MacLean's verse, and drew particular attention to the poem beginning, 'Choisich mi cuide ri mo thuigse' ('I walked with my intelligence') (Poem XXII). What attracted him, I think, was the poet's ability to converse with his intellect, and to examine human aspirations in the context of self-identity. Smith was to explore this field in great depth in the years ahead. His style was generally barer, less traditionally Gaelic in some respects, than that of Sorley MacLean, but the particularly sharp, spare dialogue used by MacLean in Poem XXII is close to Smith's voice. This volume of original poems and translations represents a harmony of styles, reflecting a particularly fruitful moment when the minds and voices of the two poets came together, and enriched one another's expression.

The corresponding interests of MacLean and Smith will be evident to readers of this book who know the works of both poets. MacLean, addressing the issues raised by the Spanish Civil War, by his love for Eimhir, and by his place in the Gaelic and global worlds of his own day, was treading a lonely and painful path which, in the years ahead, was to attract further walkers, most notably Iain Crichton Smith. Smith is pre-eminently the seeker after the 'true' nature of personal identity, in terms of religion, culture and philosophy, in local and global contexts. The 'local' perspectives were constantly challenged by the 'global' perspectives in the works of both poets. Hiroshima and Nagasaki lay only a stone's throw from Iain Crichton Smith's mental shoreline, just as the Spanish Civil War loomed over Sorley MacLean as he 'walked with [his] intelligence / beside the muted sea'.

One can trace numerous other parallels between Sorley MacLean and Iain Crichton Smith. Both poets had intensely 'local' and intensely 'global' personae. They also had a profound appreciation of physical nature, in landscape, music, art and versecraft itself. Smith appreciated the lyricism of MacLean's poetry, as well as its more sombre overtones (see his assessment of MacLean in *Towards the Human* (Edinburgh, 1986), pp. 123-31; and also his obituary, reproduced in this edition). MacLean and Smith had an equally profound awareness of the metaphysical dimensions of life, expressed in the search for identity and the discovery of the true nature of the self. It was in the interaction of such dimensions, in currents and counter-currents of thought, that their poetry gained its empowerment. This was what made them poets of outstanding stature, whose achievements were recognised far beyond the Gaelic areas. There were, of course, considerable differences between the two men and their views of the Gaelic world; Smith was much less committed to traditional Gaelic models of kinship and kindred than MacLean, though his warmth towards family and friends shines through in several poems; and his overall style was less conventional, though not without convention, Gaelic and English. Yet the broader similarities deserve recognition.

This volume commemorates two fine minds, brought together in a moment of history. It was an inspirational, unrepeatable moment. As Iain Crichton Smith comments of his translations, 'All those that I have translated I did during one period when I seemed to have a grasp of an idiom for translation and it would be difficult for me to recapture that idiom now.' In *Poems to Eimhir* we can recapture the idiom as Smith perceived it then - an idiom which united two of Scotland's most significant modern poets.

Donald E. Meek
Chief, The Gaelic Society of Inverness
December 1998

LOSS OF SORLEY MACLEAN LEAVES A GREAT GAP

Iain Crichton Smith on the great Gaelic poet
West Highland Free Press - 29.11.1996

So Sorley MacLean is dead and a great gap has opened in Gaelic and Scottish literature. One would like to have his own gift for elegy: to write one about him. For he was a great poet and a true Highlander.

As far as his poetry is concerned he and Hugh MacDiarmid were the two greatest Scottish poets of this century. What MacDiarmid did for the Scots language, Sorley did for Gaelic. Before him and in the nineteenth century Gaelic poetry had become effete, without true energy, inward-looking. With his great book, *Dàin do Eimhir*, Sorley opened the Highlands out to the wide world and to the Spanish Civil War in particular. This is a marvellous magical book of love poems.

The book is about a woman and about the Spanish Civil War to which Sorley wanted to go but couldn't because of family commitments. The tension between the love and his democratic faith and anti-fascist anger vitalised his poetry to the highest extent possible, marrying music and political thought and love in an unrepeatable amalgam.

As he himself wrote in 'Am Buaireadh':

Cha do chuir de bhuaireadh riamh
no thrioblaid dhian nam chrè
allaban Chrìosda air an talamh
neo muillionan nan speur.

This passion and turmoil illuminated his poetry and makes it stand out from the passionless poetry immediately before him.

Sorley, born in 1911, attended schools in Raasay and Portree and then took a First in English in Edinburgh University. His life-task was teaching, in Mull, Edinburgh and Plockton, and this perhaps latterly prevented him from writing much. His integrity is much to be envied. He wrote Gaelic poems as a student but it was with *Dàin do Eimhir* that he exploded like a supernova on the Scottish literary scene. This

11

book, as I have already said, seethes with the different emotions of love. And its passion made the younger generations one after the other admire him.

Involved with this love was a radical conscience. In the events in Spain he saw perhaps the despotism that had partially destroyed the Highlands at Culloden and later. He writes:

An tugadh t' fhonn no t' àilleachd ghlòrmhor
bhuam-sa gràinealachd mharbh nan dòigh seo,
a' bhruid 's am mèairleach air ceann na h-Eòrpa
's do bheul-sa uaill-dhearg, san t-seann òran?

We see this radical thrust in his great unfinished poem 'An Cuilithionn', where the mountains of Skye become a symbol for human endeavour. Here he refers to many great rebels from different countries - from Wat Tyler to the French Revolutionaries. In one of his essays he writes that the great heroes of his youth were Shelley - 'Prometheus Unbound' - and William Blake. Indeed he said that in those days he was more interersted in politics than in poetry.

In the thirties he was a Marxist and he often refers to Lenin in his poetry of that time. For someone who was brought up as a Free Presbyterian this was a huge leap. In those days he would have thought of religion as 'the opium of the masses'. And yet apart from their doctrine of the elect he had admiration for the great ministers he had heard. Thus he was fearless in following his ideas, and it is this fearlessness which breathes life into his verse. These were real difficult choices he was making.

Of course there are other MacLeans as well, the MacLean for instance of the poetry of the Second World War where he served in the African Desert and was wounded three times. Some of these poems have a Greek objectivity and sense of fate. He writes of a dead German:

Gu b' e a dheòin-san neo a chàs
a neoichiontas neo mhìorun
cha do nochd e toileachadh na bhàs
fo Dhruim Ruidhiseit.

He wouldn't be a Gaelic poet without writing about Nature and his greatest sustained poem in this field is 'Coilltean Ratharsair', with its lovely intricate imagery and music. The music of his poetry was derived from the poems of the sixteenth and seventeenth centuries which he idolised. He was indeed lucky in having parents who introduced him to the riches of Gaelic culture. The family of course was and is very talented and successful. My own headmaster in Oban was a brother of Sorley, John MacLean, a wonderful classicist and Gaelic scholar. He once told me he had been lectured to by A E Housman.

It was really after retiring from teaching that Sorley as a personality began to impinge on the reading circuit. His voice for reading was powerful and evocative; he paid more attention to the Gaelic than to the English. He didn't believe that Gaelic poetry could really be translated into English. At these readings the single poem that attracted most attention was 'Hallaig', which is about a cleared village and resonates with an eerie ghostliness in which we seem to sense the piercing depths of Highland desolation.

He was for two years a Writer in Residence at Edinburgh University. He then began to read in England and abroad. It was strange how his Gaelic poetry, though not understood by many who heard it outside the Gàidhealtachd, made a tremendous impact as at one time with students at Cambridge among many others. Honours streamed in: honorary doctorates, awards like the MacVitie and Saltire Awards, the Queen's Medal for Poetry, and others too numerous to name. It is strange that a poet in Gaelic should win the Queen's Medal for Poetry but it shows the universality of his appeal. Indeed his latest *Collected Poems* were published by Carcanet, a Manchester press.

What really can one add to what has often been said before? As a lyric poet he is supreme. He regarded the lyric as the highest form of poetry and looked for passion in it. He didn't think long poems were possible though he tried to write one in 'An Cuilithionn' which was never finished. Characteristically and generously he admitted that MacDiarmid had a variety in 'A Drunk Man Looks at the Thistle' which he could not emulate. He had the greatest regard for the lyrics of MacDiarmid and for his 'Drunk Man'. He was a friend of all the major Scottish poets. The younger Gaelic ones looked on him as their master and he was generous to them. Among Gaelic poets he refers to William Ross whom he admired greatly, and along with other famous poets, Màiri Mhòr nan Oran.

He didn't like free verse and indeed couldn't conceive of great poetry in free verse. His own poetry was very auditory and resonant with qualities of song. He was a bridge between the old poetry and the new. Latterly he didn't appear as radically revolutionary as he had at first. He loved the Highlands and remained true to his origins. He loved shinty and had played it well. He seemed ordinary in his environment, but he had lived at one time at the very tips of his senses.

Our deepest sympathy goes to his wife Renee and his two daughters; Ishbel and Mary. His wife was a rock to him in her steady temperament and common sense and ready friendliness. They were always together.

As I have said, a great gap has opened in Gaeldom. The man who was perhaps its greatest modern son has died. He derived a legacy from the past and now passes on a legacy to the future. The Highlands and his family and his many friends have been much the richer for his life.

Iain Crichton Smith

INTRODUCTION

Poems to Eimhir and Other Poems was published originally by William MacLellan of Glasgow in 1943 and had an introductory note by Douglas Young. The section 'Dàin do Eimhir' is a group of love poems: the other poems have various subject matter.

In the 'Dàin do Eimhir' section there are forty-eight poems, though they are numbered from I to LX. This means, of course, that there are a number of gaps in the original. I have not translated all the poems, and none of the Other Poems. The reasons for this are partly that one or two of them seem to me to add nothing to what has already been said in the sequence, partly that there are one or two that I found untranslatable, and partly that there are one or two that Sorley MacLean did not want translated. All those that I have translated I did during one period when I seemed to have a grasp of an idiom for the translation and it would be difficult for me to recapture exactly that idiom now.

I translated these poems (and no one knows better than myself the inadequacies of the translations) because I have felt since I first read Sorley MacLean's work that he is a major poet, but that, owing to the fact that he is writing in a minority language, very few people are able to read him. I would certainly not like these translations to be considered as definitive, only as an introduction to his work.

By a general consensus of opinion, Sorley MacLean (born 1911) is considered to be the most original poet we have had in Gaelic this century, and this for a number of reasons.

Firstly, he is profoundly original in style, though this does not at all mean that there is any loss of Gaelic atmosphere. 'Dàin do Eimhir' contains pure lyrical poems; epigrams; metaphysical poems with strong echoes of writers like John Donne; poems which depend on the double meanings of words; poems which fuse political and personal passion; poems which depend on the Highland love of place; and so on. The style therefore is sometimes pungent and aggressive, sometimes open and lyrical and free, sometimes philosophical. But in general, what unites all these poems is a committed passion which is surely rare in any poetry.

Secondly, the poems are revolutionary because they brought into Gaelic subject matter which was entirely new: and, to appreciate this properly, it is necessary to consider when they were written and under what conditions. In brief, they were written in the thirties at a time when many artists and poets were confronted by the demands of the Spanish Civil War. Out of this period came much of the best work of Auden, Spender, Day Lewis, Orwell and many other writers - as well as Lorca, Cornford and Julian Bell, to whom MacLean refers in one of his poems in the section 'Other Poems'. As well as a commitment to the democratic side in the Spanish Civil War shown in a number of the poems, there is also a commitment to Communism. Perhaps Mr. MacLean confronts this whole complex most clearly in the poem called 'Prayer' (number XVIII). It is quite reasonable to say that in no previous Gaelic poetry is there this political European commitment, though there is political commitment within the Highlands as found, for instance, in the work of Iain Lom, a poet of the seventeenth century. However, one of the important things that Sorley MacLean did was to open Gaelic poetry out to the world beyond purely parochial boundaries.

Thirdly, what is also interesting about the poet is his contemporary awareness of what commitment, or lack of it, might mean. Time and again, in these poems is found the idea that in some way or other the author's attitude to Spain is a test of what he really is, and that his love for this particular woman is also a political event, not to be dissociated from the movement of history (as, for example, in poem IV, and at the end of poem XXII). MacLean has committed himself to the 'correct' political idea, but in practice he feels he has not, and this accounts for the ending of poem XXII. In poem XXXI he addresses the great Gaelic love poet William Ross for whom he has a considerable admiration, but there is nothing of this political implication in the work of the eighteenth-century poet.

However it is as a love poet that Sorley MacLean must be judged as far as 'Dàin do Eimhir' is concerned. One often feels with Auden that when he is writing a love poem he is not addressing a real person, and that though he is a great poet his love poetry often lacks committed passion, though there is, certainly, strong intellectual passion. With Sorley MacLean one is aware first of all of the passion, and also that this is the record of a real love affair which confronted the poet with real choices in a real world. There is a constant variation of mood, a fecundity of ideas springing from the one centre.

The second poem, for instance, is built on the double meaning in Gaelic of the word 'ciall', which can mean either 'love' or 'wisdom', and the whole poem is generated from that in a metaphysical manner. Poem III introduces a political content. Poem IV specifies this political content more clearly by asking whether private love is viable in a time of political turmoil, and uses adjectives freely in a traditional Gaelic way in the description of the girl. Poem XVII uses spatial imagery to lead up to the fine last line where the whole light of a universe blazes from the face of the loved one. In XVIII we are brought face to face with the doubleness, the division: should one sacrifice the private love for the public responsibility? Poem XXII combines a metaphysical opening with a very Gaelic, almost balladic, content. XXIX is an almost surrealistic poem, while XXX is openly political with a nice ironic argument. XLII shows the Highland love of locality and XLV is again openly metaphysical. XLVIII proceeds along a series of paradoxes, while XLIX has a beautiful melodic open movement. LVII is more philosophical, and not to my mind as successful as the others. Sorley MacLean seems to me never to be really powerful when he is being intellectual without passion. However, this is rare.

It is clear, therefore, that what we have here is a set of love poems which draws on the total resources of a whole man, both in experience and in reading. The Highlands were lucky at the time the poems were written to have a writer like Sorley MacLean, a poet prepared by technical accomplishment, intelligence and ironic self-awareness to grapple with the issues of his time at their most intense, at a moment too which tested his whole human resources to their limit.

It seems to me that here in process of formation we have a new kind of Highland consciousness, brought to the complexities and dialectic of history and immersing itself in their element. It is astonishing that a Highlander brought up in such a narrow world (though broadened by a liberal education at Edinburgh University) should not have succumbed in the furnace of Communist ideology, a love affair of great intensity, and a cause demanding decision of poets and artists. It is precisely this creative confusion which produced the poetry: one feels that no other combination of factors would have been enough. It produced a union of the sophisticated and the primitive, of the intelligence and the passions, which is quite unique in Gaelic literature. It probably will not happen again in the conceivable future. That it should have happened at all seems little short of miraculous.

Iain Crichton Smith
January 1971

I

A nighean a' chùil ruaidh òir,
fada bhuat, a luaidh, mo thòir;
a nighean a' chùil ruaidh òir,
gur fada bhuat-sa mo bhròn.

Mi nochd air linne Ratharsair
's mo làmh air an stiùir,
a' ghaoth gu neo-airstealach a' crathadh an t-siùil,
mo chridhe gu balbh, cràiteach an dèidh do chiùil,
an là an-diugh 's a-màireach coingeis ri mo dhùil.

Ciar an ceò èalaidh air Dùn Cana,
frionasach garbh shliabh is canach,
a' ghaoth an iar air aghaidh mara,
dh'fhalbh mo dhùil is dùiseal tharam.

Am bristeadh geal gu làr an tuinn,
a' ghaoth na sgal mu bhàrr a' chrainn,
ach sèideadh sgal chan eil mo shuim
ri cath a dhùisgeas air muir luim.

A nighean a' chùil ruaidh òir,
fada bhuat, a luaidh, mo thòir;
a nighean a' chùil ruaidh òir,
gur glè fhada bhuat mo bhròn.

I

Girl of the gold-yellow hair,
Indifferent, to you, is my desire;
Girl of the gold-yellow hair,
Indifferent, to you, this patient fire.

Tonight on the floods of Ratharsair,
My distant hand rests on the tiller.
Not languid is the wind that shakes the sails.
Languid my heart because your music fails.
Becalmed my sea where no large wind prevails.

Round dark Dùn Cana soundless mists are creeping
Angry the grasses on the mountains sloping.
The western wind across the sea unsleeping.
This is the death of dreaming and of hoping.

Around the masts the barren winds are shrieking.
Before the boat the whitening waves are breaking.
But let the wind be fierce and masts be creaking,
What do I care for battles of their making?

Girl of the gold-yellow hair,
Indifferent, to you, is my desire;
Girl of the gold-yellow hair,
Indifferent, to you, this patient fire.

II

A CHIALL 'S A GHRAIDH

Ma thubhairt ar cainnt gu bheil an ciall
Co-ionann ris a' ghaol,
Chan fhìor dhi.

Nuair dhearc mo shùil air t' aodann
Cha d' nochd e ciall a' ghràidh,
Cha d' fheòraich mi mun trian ud.

Nuair chuala mi do ghuth cha d' rinn
E an roinneadh seo nam chrè;
Cha d' rinn a' chiad uair.

Ach dhiùchd siud dhomh gun aithne dhomh
Is reub e freumh mo chrè,
Gam sguabadh leis na shiaban.

Leis na bha dhomh de bhreannachadh
Gun d' rinn mi faileas strì;
Gun d' rinneadh gleac lem chèill.

Bho dhoimhneachd an t-seann ghliocais seo
'S ann labhair mi rim ghaol:
'Cha diù leam thu, cha diù bhuam'.

    Air an taobh a-staigh mo ghaol,
    Mo thuigse air an taobh ghrinn,
    Is bhristeadh a' chòmhla bhaoth.

Is thubhairt mo thuigse ri mo ghaol,
'Cha dhuinn an dùbailteachd;
Tha an coimeasgadh sa ghaol.'

II

And if our language says that love
And reason are the same
She's lying.

When first your beauty struck my eyes
They did not learn to be wise,
They weren't scholars of such terms.

When first I heard your voice, my clay
Was not sundered in this way,
Not the first time.

The assault was more indirect
Against my heart and intellect.
Later, the storm grew strong.

With all I had of prudence
I fought in my defence.
I used sagacious eloquence.

And from my ancient wisdom I
Spoke from the chaos of my sky:
"I do not want you here nor yet away."

My love was on the inside,
My wisdom remained outside,
That thin partition was destroyed.

And reason spoke to my love thus:
"How foolish is this doubleness.
Love is the reason we possess."

III

Cha do chuir de bhuaireadh riamh
no thrioblaid dhian nam chrè
allaban Chrìosda air an talamh
no muillionan nan speur.

'S cha d' ghabh mi suim de aisling bhaoith -
coille uaine tìr an sgeòil -
mar leum mo chridhe rag ri tuar
a gàire 's cuailein òir.

Agus chuir a h-àilleachd sgleò
air bochdainn 's air creuchd sheirbh
agus air saoghal tuigse Leninn,
air fhoighidinn 's air fheirg.

III

Never was I so tormented
or troubled in my clay
by Christ's wanderings on the earth,
or the millions of the sky:

and I gave no heed to that silly dream -
the woods of a far air -
as my stiff heart melted in the power
of her laughter and golden hair.

And her beauty laid a shadow on
poverty and our bitter birth,
on Lenin's intellectual world,
his patience and his wrath.

IV

A nighean a' chùil bhuidhe, throm-bhuidh, òr-bhuidh,
fonn do bheòil-sa 's gaoir na h-Eòrpa,
a nighean gheal chasurlach aighearach bhòidheach,
cha bhiodh masladh ar latha-ne searbh nad phòig-sa.

An tugadh t' fhonn no t' àilleachd ghlòrmhor
bhuam-sa gràinealachd mharbh nan dòigh seo,
a' bhrùid 's am mèairleach air ceann na h-Eòrpa
's do bheul-sa, uaill-dhearg, san t-seann òran?

An tugadh corp geal is clàr grèine
bhuam-sa cealgaireachd dhubh na brèine,
nimh bhùirdeasach is puinnsean crèide
is dìblidheachd ar n-Albann èitigh?

An cuireadh bòidhchead is ceòl suaimhneach
bhuamsa breòiteachd an adhbhair bhuain seo,
am mèinear Spàinnteach a' leum ri cruadal
is anam mòrail dol sìos gun bhruaillean?

Dè bhiodh pòg do bheòil uaibhrich
mar ris gach braon den fhuil luachmhoir
a thuit air raointean reòta fuara
nam beann Spàinnteach bho fhòirne cruadhach?

Dè gach cuach ded chual òr-bhuidh
ris gach bochdainn, àmhghar 's dòrainn
a thig 's a thàinig air sluagh na h-Eòrpa
bho Long nan Daoine gu daors' a' mhòr-shluaigh?

IV

Girl of the yellow, heavy-yellow, gold-yellow hair,
the tune of your lips and Europe's pain together.
Lustrous, ringletted, joyful, beautiful lass,
our time's shame would not infect your kiss.

Can the music of your beauty hide from me
the ominous discord in this harmony?
The rampant thief and brute at Europe's head,
the ancient songs, your lips so proud and red.

Can a body's whiteness and a forehead's sun
conceal that impudent treachery from my brain -
spite of the bourgeoisie, poison of its creed,
a dismal Scotland, feeble and weak-kneed?

Can beauty and the mendacity of verse
deceive the patient with its transient cures
or hide the Spanish miner from his doom,
his soul going down without delirium?

What is your kiss, electrical and proud,
when valued by each drop of precious blood
that fell on the frozen mountain-sides of Spain
when men were dying in their bitter pain?

What is each ringlet of your golden hair
when weighed against that poverty and fear
which Europe's people bear and still must bear
from the first slave-ship to slavery entire?

VIII

The innocent and the beautiful
have no enemy but time.

W. B. Yeats

Bha dùil leam gun do chreid mi bhuat-sa
briathran cuimir an duain ud;
agus ar leam nach do shaoil mi
gu faicinn aomadh an cluaine.

Ach thuig mi gum b' fhaoin do smuain-sa
nuair chunnaic mi an Di-luain sin
le m' shùilean fhìn an clogad stàilinn
air ceann àlainn mo luaidhe.

VIII

The innocent and the beautiful
have no enemy but time.

W. B. Yeats

I thought I understood from you
that these lines were exact and true,
nor did I think that I would find
their falsehood bitter in my mind.

But that plausible epigram
proved itself another dream
when on that Monday I saw with dread
the steel helmet on your golden head.

XI

Tric 's mi gabhail air Dùn Eideann
baile glas gun ghathadh grèine,
's ann a lasadh e led bhòidhche,
baile lòghmhor, geal-reultach.

XI

Often walking quite alone
Edinburgh's grey sunless stone
it would flash with your sudden rays
white-starred, uniquely precious.

XIV

REIC ANAMA

Bàrd a' strì ri càs an t-saoghail,
siùrsachd bhuadhan is an daorsa
leis na mhealladh mòr-roinn dhaoine,
cha mhise fear a chanadh, shaoil leam,
gun tugadh reic an anama faochadh.

Ach thubhairt mi rium fhìn, 's cha b' aon-uair,
gu reicinn m' anam air do ghaol-sa
nam biodh feum air brèig is aomadh.
Thubhairt mi an deifir sin gun smaointinn
gum b' e an toibheum dubh 's an claonadh.

Do mhaitheanas dhomh airson na smuaine
gum b' thusa tè a ghabhadh truaghan
de spiorad beag lag suarach
a ghabhadh reic, eadhan air buadhan
t' aodainn àlainn 's do spioraid uallaich.

Uime sin, their mi rithist, an dràsta,
gu reicinn m' anam air do sgàth-sa
dà uair, aon uair air son t' àilleachd
agus uair eile airson a' ghràis ud,
nach gabhadh tu spiorad reicte tràilleil.

XIV

Poet struggling under strain,
corruption of gifts and the cheap chain
which has enticed so many men:
surely not I, not I, would cry:
Surrender gives relief from pain.

But I have said (this isn't new)
that I would sell my soul for you
(not false to love though to the rest untrue).
Yet that was blasphemy, I see it now,
that was a heresy love led me to.

Forgive me therefore for that sordid thought
that you, my dear, could possibly accept
a wretch dishonoured and dispirited:
that you could watch, indifferent, the sale
for even your love of honesty and wit.

And therefore I will say it yet again:
I'd sell my soul for you, my heart's queen
not once but twice: the first time for your keen
beauty: and the second time because
you would not take a soul so small and mean.

XVII

Lìonmhorachd anns na speuran,
òr-chriathar muillionan de reultan,
fuar, fad as, lòghmhor, àlainn,
tosdach, neo-fhaireachdail, neo-fhàilteach.

Lànachd an eòlais m' an cùrsa,
failmhe an aineolais gun iùl-chairt,
cruinne-cè a' gluasad sàmhach,
aigne leatha fhèin san àrainn.

Chan iadsan a ghluais mo smaointean,
chan e mìorbhail an iomchair aognaidh,
chan eil a' mhìorbhail ach an gaol duinn,
soillse cruinne an lasadh t' aodainn.

XVII

Tumultuous plenty in the heavens,
gold-sieve of a million stars,
cold, distant, blazing, splendid,
silent and callous in their course.

Fullness of knowledge in their going,
an empty, chartless, ignorant plain.
A universe in soundless motion.
A brooding intellect alone.

It was not they who woke my thinking.
It was not the miracle of their grave
fearful procession, but your face,
a naked universe of love.

XVIII

URNAIGH

A chionn nach eil dìon ann
agus a chionn nach eil m' iarrtas
ach na fhaileas faoin sgialachd,
chan eil ann ach: Dèanam làidir
m' aigne fhìn an aghaidh àmhghair.

Oir chunnaic mi an Spàinn caillte,
sealladh a rinn mo shùilean saillte,
agus gaoir a chuir maille
air iomchar mo chridhe àrdain
le neoinitheachd is bàs nan sàr fhear.

Chì sinn a-rithist an dràsta
claoidh cridhe 's bàs an àrdain
agus neoinitheachd neo-àghmhor
anns gach dòchas treun faoilidh
len sgarar sinn bhon bhàs aognaidh.

Bha seo aig Còrnford òg na ghaisge,
eagal smuain a ghaoil bhith faisg air
nuair bha an Spàinn na latha-traisg dha,
eagal a challa air an duine,
eagal an eagail air a' churaidh.

Dè an t-eagal a bhios ormsa
ro thuiltean aognaidh an onfhaidh
a-nis on chuala mi am monmhar?
Theirear gum faicear trom-laighe,
am bàs 's a' ghort a' tachdadh aighir;

XVIII

Now that the ivory towers are down
and my desire is but a thin
shade of a tale that's dead and gone,
there is only: Let me strengthen
my own spirit against pain.

For I have watched while Spain, struck dead,
salted the eyes within my head
and slowed my wheels of pride and blood,
with thoughts of nothingness and death
and heroes who have lost their breath.

And now we see on every side
heart-break and the death of pride,
the nothingness that will deride
every generous thought we nursed
to satisfy the spirit's thirst.

Cornford in his heroic day
prayed that his love would not betray
Spain and her cross of agony -
Cornford afraid his love was near,
Cornford afraid of his fear.

What of my fear? Can I sustain
the torments that will pierce my brain
now that I've heard the storms begin?
They say that nightmares now annoy
and deadly famine strangles joy,

gum faicear a' ghort air na raointean,
an èislig chumhachadh na caoile,
a bheir a' bheatha is an gaol bhuainn,
a leagas sìos a dh'ionnsaigh uaghach
le acras is eu-dòchas neo-uallach.

Ach saoil sibh an dèan mi ùrnaigh
rim spiorad fhìn an aghaidh m' ùidhe,
stad mo chridhe, dalladh shùilean?
An guidh mi do ghaol bhith air a shracadh
à friamhaichean mo chridhe thachdte?

An iarr mi mo chridhe bhith glainte
bho annfhannachd mo ghaoil ghlain ghil?
An iarr mi spiorad 's e air fhaileadh
eadhan gum faighear anns a' bhoile mi
cho treun ri Dimitrov no ri Ó Conghaile?

Tha mi a' tuigsinn an dràsta
gun tàinig lìonsgaradh sa chàs seo,
gleac a' chinne-daonna neo-bhàsmhoir,
an neach mu choinneamh roghainn sàr-chruaidh,
bàs 's a' bheatha bhiothbhuain no beatha bhàsail.

Mo bheatha-sa a' bheatha bhàsail
a chionn nach d' fhail mi cridhe mo shàth-ghaoil,
a chionn gun tug mi gaol àraidh,
a chionn nach sgarainn do ghràdh-sa
's gum b' fheàrr leam boireannach na 'n Eachdraidh fhàsmhor.

Chunnaic mi 'n fhuil chraobhach ag èirigh,
tein-aighir an spioraid air na slèibhtean,
an saoghal truagh a' call a chreuchdan:
thuig is thùr mi fàth an langain
ged nach robh mo chridhe air fhaileadh.

that hunger walks about the earth
with solemn ghosts of thirst and dearth
cropping our tender lives at birth
and forcing to the low grave
all our arrogance and love.

And do you think that I will pray
against the terrors of my way?
(Stopping of heart and blinded eye.)
That you, my love, be wrenched and torn
from the bitter roots where you were born?

That thus I might be purified
from the infirmity in my side.
Or should I pray for a soul arrayed
in blood and battle, proudly dressed
like Dimitrov, Connolly and the rest?

Today I clearly understand
the gulf that cracks across the mind,
strife on behalf of human-kind,
the choice that catches at our breath,
immortal dying or a living death.

Mine is a hopeless death alive
because I did not force my love
out of my splendid private grove,
because when History strode by
I loved a woman in my secret sky.

I saw blood beating like a pulse,
the spirit's lightning on the hills,
the poor world shedding all its ills,
I understood with a heart impure
the language of the wounded deer.

Esan dh' am bheil an cridhe air ionnlaid
thèid e tro theine gun tionndadh;
dìridh e bheinn mhòr gun ionndrainn;
cha d' fhuair mise leithid de dh'anam
's mo chridhe ach air leth-fhaladh.

'S e 'n ùrnaigh seo guidhe na duilghe,
an guidhe toibheumach neo-iomlan,
guidhe cam coirbte an tionndaidh,
an guidhe gun dèan mi guidhe,
gun ghuidhe 'n t-susbaint a ruigheachd.

Chuala mi mu bhàs neo-aoibhneach
agus mu acras gorta oillteil
a' tighinn an tòrachd na foille.
Ciamar a sheasas mi rim marc-shluagh
's gun mo chridhe ach leth fhailte?

An uair tha 'n spiorad air fhaileadh
caillidh e gach uile fhaileas,
caillidh e gach uile fhannachd.
Ach cò a ghabhas air mo gheal ghaol
aomadh, fannachd no faileas?

Cha ruigear a leas ceistear no sgrùdair
a dh'fhaicinn nach eil nam ùrnaigh
a' Ghairm Eifeachdach no 'n Dùrachd,
's ged tha mi soilleir anns an fhìrinn
nach eil mo spiorad aon-fhillte.

A chionn nach cuirear coire air diathan,
nach eil ach nam faileas iarraidh
agus a sheachnadh an duine Crìosda,
chan eil mo chaomhachd ris an Nàdar
a thug an tuigse shoilleir shlàn dhomh,
an eanchainn shingilte 's an cridhe sgàinte.

He whose heart is cleansed and pure
will walk unswerving through the fire,
will climb huge hills and never tire,
but mine is not the hero's part,
who live with a corrupted heart.

And this, the prayer you hear me pray,
is vain and blasphemous and dry,
corrupt and crooked and awry,
a prayer to pray and nothing more,
the shadow of a false fire.

I've heard about the death which comes
to terrify deceit and dreams
with thirst and famine in its arms.
How can I face their cruel charge
with a heart I could not learn to purge?

For when the heart is purged and clean
it can confront most bitter pain
and will not faint or suffer stain.
But who will say my white love
suffers the laughter of the grave?

There's no need for a catechist
to tell my prayer is but a ghost,
a shadowy figure in the mist,
to show me that my spirit is not
as hard and lucid as my thought.

And since the gods cannot be blamed -
being but wishes we have dreamed,
and Christ a man who walked unarmed -
I cannot worship or extol
Nature which made my intellect whole,
the single mind and the divided soul.

XIX

Thug mise dhut biothbhuantachd
is dè thug thu dhòmhsa?
Cha tug ach saighdean
geura do bhòidhchid.
Thug thu cruaidh shitheadh
is treaghaidh na dòrainn,
domblas an spioraid,
goirt dhrithleann na glòire.

Ma thug mise dhut biothbhuantachd
's tusa thug dhòmhs' i;
's tu gheuraich mo spiorad
's chuir an drithleann nam òran;
's ged rinn thu mo mhilleadh
an tuigse na còmhraig,
nam faicinn thu rithist
ghabhainn tuilleadh 's an còrr dheth.

Nam faicinn mum choinneimh
air magh Tìr na h-òige
an dèidh dìochuimhn' mo dhragha
clàr foinnidh do bhòidhchid,
b' fheàrr leam an siud e
ged thilleadh mo bhreòiteachd,
's na suaimhneas an spioraid
mi rithist bhith leòinte.

XIX

I gave you eternity
and what did you give me?
Only the bitter arrows
of your hurting beauty.
You pierced me with hard onset,
you made my days sorry
with vinegar of the spirit,
the sore gleam of glory.

Yet the eternity I gave you
was born from you and to you belongs,
you taught my five senses
to put their brilliance in my songs:
and though you almost ruined me
for our hard historical campaign
I'd still receive, if I could have,
more of your weakening gifts again.

If I could see you standing now
on the calm plains of the Land of Youth,
I in forgetfulness of ruin,
you in your white glittering cloth,
I'd wish these days to return
when my spirit struggled (though in vain)
and, rather than defeated peace,
the battle to begin again.

A nighean bhuidhe àlainn
's ann shrac thu mo threòir-sa
agus dh'fhiaraich mo shlighe
bho shireadh mo thòrachd;
ach ma ruigeas mi m' àite,
coille àrd luchd nan òran,
's tu grìosach an dàin dhomh,
rinn thu bàrd dhìom le dòrainn.

Thog mi an calbh seo
air beinn fhalbhaich na tìme
ach 's esan clach-chuimhne
a bhios suim dheth gu dìlinn,
is ged bhios tusa aig fear-pòsda
is tu gun eòl air mo strì-sa,
's e do ghlòir-sa mo bhàrdachd
an dèidh cnàmhachd do lìthe.

O most beautiful white girl,
you tore my intellect apart,
you made my journey crooked
and drew me from my single art.
Yet should I ever reach that wood
where poems burn along each leaf,
you were the author of my songs
you made a bard of me with grief.

I've built you a tall monument
on the crumpling mountains of our time,
yet this is a memorial
that men will speak of when you're dumb,
and though I lose you, and another
enjoy you to his every wish
you'll blaze and glitter in my songs
after the setting of your flesh.

XX

Nan robh an comas mar a b' àill leam,
le ealain fuaighte ri mo shàth-ghaol,
chan e naoi deug an àireamh
no a leithid seo de dhàintean
a choisriginn do t' aodann àlainn
agus dod spiorad uallach gràsmhor.
Chan e ach dàintean sam fuaigheadh
ceòl is caoine is smuaintean
is mac-meanmna na mhìorbhail
le dianas grèine 's iomaluas iarmailt,
ciùin mar chamhanaich na h-oidhche
's caoin mar bhristeadh latha boillsgeadh
agus ùr mar thoiseach aoibhneis,
dàintean luathghaireach gun shireadh,
doimhne, fìnealta, le mire,
dàintean sam faighte singilt'
buadhan an triùir 's iad fillte,
dàintean sam faicte chrois
bh' air Yeats is Blok is Uilleam Ros.

XX

If my capacity were such
that love and intelligence would match,
it's not nineteen songs I would have made
consecrate to your flowing grace
and spirit abundant with its pride.
Not these but songs that would be woven
of music, intellect, holy passion,
miraculous imagination,
the sun's vehemence, stars motion,
songs as tranquil as the night,
as splendid as the morning's bright
rising: or as break of joy,
profound songs, exultant, gay,
songs woven of great words
like the high trinity of bards,
songs containing the great cross
of Yeats, Blok and William Ross.

William Ross: Gaelic Love-poet of the eighteenth century.

Died young of consumption.

XXI

Dè dhòmhsa m' àite
am measg bàird na h-Albann
ged chuireas mi an Gàidhlig
loinn is àilleachd fhalbhach?
Cha tuig thusa mo ghràdh bhuam
no m' àrdan arraghlòir,
a nighean bhuidhe àlainn,
ge tu m' àilleachd fhalbhach.

XXI

What is my place to me
Among the Scottish bards
Though I should fix a mortal beauty
In my Gaelic words?
You will not understand my love
Nor my boastful arrogant delight,
Lovely yellow-haired girl,
It's of your dying that I write.

'Choisich mi cuide ri mo thuigse
a-muigh ri taobh a' chuain:
bha sinn còmhla ach bha ise
a' fuireach tiotan bhuam'

XXII

Choisich mi cuide ri mo thuigse
a-muigh ri taobh a' chuain:
bha sinn còmhla ach bha ise
a' fuireach tiotan bhuam.

An sin thionndaidh i ag ràdh:
A bheil e fìor gun cual
thu gu bheil do ghaol geal àlainn
a' pòsadh tràth Di-luain?

Bhac mi 'n cridhe bha 'g èirigh
nam bhroilleach reubte luath
is thubhairt mi: Tha mi cinnteach;
carson bu bhreug e bhuam?

Ciamar a smaoinichinn gun glacainn
an rionnag leugach òir,
gum beirinn oirre 's gun cuirinn i
gu ciallach na mo phòc?

Cha d' ghabh mise bàs croinn-ceusaidh
an èiginn chruaidh na Spàinn
is ciamar sin bhiodh dùil agam
ri aon duais ùir an dàin?

Cha do lean mi ach an t-slighe chrìon,
bheag, ìosal, thioram, thlàth:
is ciamar sin a choinnichinn
ri bheithir-theine 'ghràidh?

Ach nan robh 'n roghainn rithist dhomh
's mi 'm sheasamh air an àird,
leumainn a nèamh no Iutharna
le spiorad 's cridhe slàn.

XXII

I walked with my intelligence
beside the muted sea:
we were together, but it kept
a little distance from me.

And then it turned and spoke these words:
"Is it the truth that I have heard
that your white lovely darling
on Monday will be wed?"

I checked the bitter heart that rose
in my swift torn side
and answered: "It is certain.
Why should I have lied?"

How could I think that I could catch
that jewelled golden star
and place it in a prudent purse
where my wise treasures are?

I who avoided the sore cross
and agony of Spain,
what should I expect or hope,
what splendid prize to win?

I who took the coward's way,
the mean road of the slave,
how should I expect to meet
the thunderbolt of love?

Yet, if I had a second chance,
still standing proud and tall,
I'd jump with undivided heart
from heaven or from hell.

XXIII

Bodhar, neo-shuaimhneach, am feirg,
àmhghar an cridhe na mòrachd,
binneas ceòl camhanaich nan eun,
òg mhadainn ceòl Bheethoven.

A luaidh, anns an talla dhlùth,
balbh fo ealain ùir an t-sàr fhir,
dhiùchd còmhla fa chomhair mo rùin
gathadh a' chiùil is t' àilleachd.

A nighean, a nighean bhàn,
dh'fhilleadh an ceòl mòr nad àilleachd,
shuaineadh a' chòisir mhòr nad loinn,
bhàrc an taigh mòr lem ghràdh-sa.

Dhùin mo shùilean ris a' cheòl
a bha air tòrachd an èibhneis,
dhiùchd Diana an cloich chaoimh
agus Deirdre taobh Loch Eite.

B' e t' ìomhaigh-sa agus an ceòl
a chruinnich còmhlan nan leugach,
chuir Deirdre do Ghleann Da Ruadh,
Diana an ruaig nan Greugach.

Nighean, a nighean mo luaidh,
b' e aoibhneas a' chiùil mhòir t' aodann,
Beethoven agus Maol Donn
air magh lom cridhe sgaoilte.

Bodhar, neo-shuaimhneach, am feirg,
àmhghar, allaban a' Cheòlraidh:
geal, àlainn, socair le uaill chiùin
an nighean ùr na bòidhche.

XXIII

Deaf and restless the rage,
sorrow stinging the noble heart,
music of a dawn of birds,
morning of Beethoven's art.

Darling, in the packed hall,
speechless beneath the music's power,
the two were helplessly fused,
your beauty and that piercing air.

Girl, O fair-haired girl,
you were woven into that grave
and royal melody. The house
was bursting with my ardent love.

My eyes were closed against that music
which sought its harmony through pain,
I thought of Deirdre by Glen Etive,
Diana of the calm stone.

That company of glittering jewels
was born from the music and your cheeks.
They sent Deirdre to Glendaruel
and brought Diana to the Greeks.

Girl, girl of my eulogy,
the joy of the music was your face,
Beethoven and the great pibroch
sprang from my heart's level place.

Deaf and restless the anger,
tormented wandering of a mind:
white and brilliant your beauty
seated at my left hand.

An cuirear gu cuimir suas
anns a' cho-chur cluaineis saoghail,
ànradh an duine mhòir 's an truaigh
agus ciùin luathghair t' aodainn?

An dèanar a' cho-chur den dàn,
de thruaighe 's de ghlòir na cruinne,
a' bhrèine bhreòite, oillteil, thruagh,
t' àilleachd is uaisle luinneag?

Thachd an fhiabhras iomadh truagh
's dh'fhàg i iomadh athair breòite,
ach dh'fhàg ceòl cumha Phàdraig Mhòir
àmhghar a chloinne glòrmhor.

Bhàsaich an truaighe gun sgleò
leanabh is seann duine còmhla,
agus cha tàinig ceòl no dàn
a chur àilleachd air dòrainn.

Deirdre ghuanach anns an uaigh
anns an t-Sìorraidheachd gun shireadh,
agus mo ghaol sa chòisir mhòir
buadhmhor thar luathghair filidh.

Cha dèanar a' cho-chur den chàs,
glòir agus ànradh na cruinne,
an èitig fhiabhrais 's Pàdraig Mòr,
daorsa, Beethoven 's thusa.

Bodhar, neo-shuaimhneach, am feirg,
ceòl binn, gailleannach, ciùin, glòrmhor,
geal, àlainn, socair, gun aon ghiamh,
gun bharrachd fiamh do bhòidhche.

Can there be offered tidily,
in a woven synthesis, his distress -
the anguish of a great spirit -
the joyful calmness of your face?

Can such a synthesis be woven
from human wretchedness and wrong -
impudence, rotten, unashamed:
your beauty in a proud song?

Fever has throttled many a hero,
leaving his descendants bare -
but the music of his elegy
transformed his flesh to a blazing star.

Yet many a wretched one is dead -
the pauper and the feverish child.
Who has written their elegies
to make the heart fierce and wild?

Capricious Deirdre's in her grave -
in Eternity without a word.
My love is woven in the music
priceless beyond praise of bard.

Such synthesis is dream indeed -
of the planet's glory and its pain,
the hero's feverish death and you,
Beethoven and the slave's chain.

Deaf and restless the rage,
vehement music, glorious, clear.
Impeccable your brilliant beauty,
flawless in its perfect air.

XXIV

Nuair thubhairt thu nach robh bhòidhche
ach cosamhlach is le fàiling
's ann bha mise smaointinn:
saoil, òinseach àlainn,
an cainte sin ri Naoise
nuair thaobh e Earra-Ghàidheal?

XXIV

When you remarked that beauty
and weakness are the same,
it's then that I was thinking:
Could epigrams, dear fool,
have spoken so to Naoise
as he approached Argyll?

XXVII.

Thubhairt an sgrùdair gun robh m' ealain
a' dol gu laomadh le meallan
drithleannach, foinnidh, caoireach.
Ach, a ghaoil, 's ann bhod aodann
a fhuair i mealladh a leugachd,
a fhuair i ceòl-gàire h-èibhneis,
a fhuair i suaimhneas a h-aogais.

XXVII

The reader told me my imagination
was gathering to a conflagration,
lustrous, brilliant and clear.
But, dearest, it was your face
that fashioned this astounding grace,
you are the origin of the force
and abundant constancies of my verse.

'An t-Sìorraidheachd Fhalamh Fhàsail'

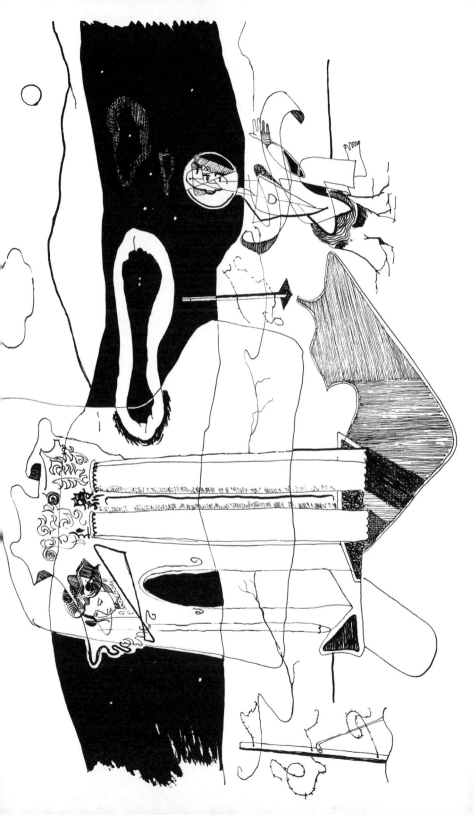

XXVIII

NA SAMHLAIDHEAN

Nan robh mi air do ghaol fhaotainn
theagamh nach biodh aig mo dhàintean
an t-sìorraidheachd fhalamh fhàsail,
a' bhiothbhuantachd a tha an dàn dhaibh.
'S ann, a ghaoil, bho na taobhan
fad às, cianail a bhios an glaodhaich,
ag iargan, ag èigheach air do ghaol-sa.
Gabhaidh iad mullaichean nan àrd-bheann
ginealach, a' sìor rànaich,
a' sìor iargain do ghràidh-sa,
a' sìor dhèanamh luaidh air t' àilleachd:
falbhaidh iad nochdta air sràidean
na h-Eachdraidh agus na Bàrdachd:
chithear iad air rathaidean àrda
nan cridheachan a' sìor mhàrsail:
tachraidh iad anns an oidhche
ris na bàird nan suaineadh loinn-gheal:
ni iad caithris solas choinnleir;
cha mhùch bristeadh fàire 'm boillsgeadh.
Seasaidh iad mun chiste-laighe
far a bheil a' chrè na laighe,
crè ghlas gaol nam bàrd gun aighear:
seasaidh iad thar na h-uaghach,
gun rudhadh, glaisneulach an gruaidhean.

Falbhaidh iad nan ròs air slèibhtean
far bheil grian nam bàrd ag èirigh.

XXVIII

Perhaps if I had won your love
my songs wouldn't have known the grave
empty eternity they'll have.
Their cries will be from a far place
pleading and yearning for your grace.
They'll be infesting the high hills
of generations with vain howls.

They will go naked on the way
of History and Poetry:
they will be seen on the steep height
of the heart marching: and at night
be met by poets swathed in white.
They will keep candle-vigil
nor by the morning be made dull.
They'll stand by the silent chest
where the burnt bodies are at rest,
the bodies of the joyless bards:
they'll stand by the graves of the great dead.
The blossoms of their cheeks are shed.

They will be roses on the horizon
where the sun of poetry is blazing.

XXIX

COIN IS MADAIDHEAN-ALLAIDH

Thar na sìorraidheachd, thar a sneachda,
chì mi mo dhàin neo-dheachdte,
chì mi lorgan an spòg a' breacadh
gile shuaimhneach an t-sneachda;
calg air bhoile, teanga fala,
gadhair chaola 's madaidhean-allaidh,
a' leum thar mullaichean nan gàrradh,
a' ruith fo sgàil nan craobhan fàsail,
a' gabhail cumhang nan caol-ghleann,
a' sireadh caisead nan gaoth-bheann;
an langan gallanach a' sianail
thar loman cruaidhe nan àm cianail,
an comhartaich bhiothbhuan na mo chluasan,
an deann-ruith a' gabhail mo bhuadhan:
rèis nam madadh 's nan con iargalt
luath air tòrachd an fhiadhaich,
tro na coilltean gun fhiaradh,
thar mullaichean nam beann gun shiaradh;
coin chiùine cuthaich mo bhàrdachd,
madaidhean air tòir na h-àilleachd,
àilleachd an anama 's an aodainn,
fiadh geal thar bheann is raointean,
fiadh do bhòidhche ciùine, gaolaich,
fiadhach gun sgur gun fhaochadh.

XXIX

Across eternity, across her snows
I see my undictated songs:
I see the traces of their paws
dappling the whiteness of the snows,
bristles in tumult, blood on their tongues.
Slender wolves and slender dogs,
leaping across walls and dykes,
hurrying below barren twigs,
taking the narrow paths of glens,
seeking the sheer and windy hills.
Hear the music of their wails
on the harsh levels of our time,
eternal barking in my ears.
This pace is tearing at my mind.
Race of the terrible dogs and wolves
hard on the tender tracks of deer,
straight through the woods without veering,
straight to the summits without sheering,
the mild furious dogs of poetry,
wolves on the single track of beauty,
beauty of face, beauty of soul,
the white deer on plain and hill,
deer of your beauty, calm and bright,
they're hunting you by day and night.

XXX

'S mi 'm Bhoilseabhach nach tug suim
riamh do bhànrainn no do rìgh,
nan robh againn Alba shaor,
Alba co-shìnte ri ar gaol,
Alba gheal bheadarrach fhaoil,
Alba àlainn shona laoch,
gun bhùirdeasachd bhig chrìon bhaoith,
gun sgreamhalachd luchd na maoin',
gun chealgaireachd oillteil chlaoin,
Alba aigeannach nan saor,
Alba ar fala, Alba ar gaoil,
bhristinn lagh dligheach nan rìgh,
bhristinn lagh cinnteach shaoi,
dh'èighinn nad bhànrainn Albann thu
neo-ar-thaing na Poblachd ùir.

XXX

Though I'm a Bolshevik who would never sing
my high praises for queen or king,
if we had only Scotland free,
Scotland extended lovingly
in the bed of hospitality,
Scotland, of brave tranquillity,
Scotland without its bourgeoisie,
without its loathsome, miserly,
depraved, ugly treachery,
Scotland, heroic, spirited,
Scotland as dear as our own blood -
if Scotland were such I'd break the fiat
of our new proletariat,
and in spite of their spite - or a king's spleen -
I'd crown you, of such Scotland, queen.

XXXI

Uilleim Rois, dè chanamaid
a' coinneachadh taobh thall a' bhàis?
Dhèanainn luaidh air t' Oran Eile;
dè theireadh tusa mu na dàin
a sgaoil mi ealain-shriante,
eachraidh fhiadhaich bhàrd?

XXXI

William Ross, what would we say
in the strange encounter of the dead?
I would mention your Oran Eile.
What would you say about the herd
I bridled in my artistry -
the fierce cavalry of a bard?

Oran Eile : Literally, another song. One of Ross's.

XXXII

Sgatham le faobhar-roinn gach àilleachd
a' chuir do bhòidhche nam bhàrdachd;
's dèanam dàin cho lom aognaidh
ri bàs Liebknecht no daorsa;
loisgeam gach meanglan craoibhe
a dh'fhàs aoibhneach thar duilghe
's cuiream deuchainn an t-sluaigh
an iarann-cruadhach mo dhuain.

XXXII

Let me lop from my verse every grace
shed by the lustre of your face,
and let it learn the economy
of Liebknecht's death and slavery:
let me burn away each leaf
that grew joyfully from my grief.
And let me hammer the people's wrongs
into the iron of my songs.

' 's eòl dhomh seirbheachd gheur an spioraid
nas fhèarr na aoibhneas luath a' chridhe'

XXXIII

Chan eil freasdal nam bàrd
dealaichte bho fhreasdal chàich:
bha 'm fortan le Donnchadh Bàn
is fhuair Uilleam Ros a shàth
den àmhghar, den chaitheamh 's den bhàs.

XXXIV.

An uair a labhras mi mu aodann
agus mu spiorad geal mo ghaoil ghil
's ann a theireadh neach nach d' ràinig
mo shùilean dalla air a' chàthar,
air a' bhoglaich oillteil ghrànda
sam bheil a' bhùirdeasachd a' bàthadh:
ach chunnaic mi bho àird a' Chuilithinn
gathadh glòir is breòiteachd duilghe:
chunnaic mi òradh lainnir grèine
agus boglach dhubh na brèine:
's eòl dhomh seirbheachd gheur an spioraid
nas fheàrr na aoibhneas luath a' chridhe.

XXXIII

Not different the fate of bards
from those who do not work with words.
Luck was on Macintyre's side
but William Ross was edified
with pain and consumption till he died.

XXXIV

When I speak of a loved face
and a spirit abundant with its grace
someone might say: Your dialogue
reveals no knowledge of that bog
of ugliness and low cunning
where the fat bourgeoisie are drowning.
But I have seen from the Cuillins' height
a marsh pierced by a glorious light:
I've seen them both, gold radiance
and the black bog of insolence.
The darkening sourness of the spirit -
not joy - is what I most inherit.

Duncan Ban Macintyre is considered by many to be the greatest of
Gaelic poets. He lived in the eighteenth century, and is best known for
his long poem on Ben Dorain, a mountain in Perthshire. He served as
gamekeeper in this area. Later he went to Edinburgh where he died
after a long life.

XXXV

Thig am chomhair, oidhche chiùin,
gorm reultachd adhair agus driùchd,
ged nach glanar bho aon àird
bochdainn saoghail, gaoir na Spàinn:
oidhche is Maol Donn a' seinn
ceòl mòr ciùine air a' bheinn,
oidhche is mo ghaol na lì,
oidhche air nach fhaicear mi
lem shùilean fhìn, a chionn lànachd,
a' cur dubhair air an fhàire:
thig am chomhair gorm, cruinn,
is cuireadh mi air dòigh gun shuim
gathadh ùrlair ciùil Maoil Duinn.

XXXV

Come to me, tranquil night, and you
azure of sky, sweet fall of dew,
though firmaments will never be clean
of a world's poverty, weeping Spain:
night when the pipes are playing still
their great calm music on the hill:
night with its jewels for my queen,
night on which I won't be seen
darkening a horizon with
the long shadows of my wrath:
come to me, night, so blue and calm
and I will weave the paradigm
of the pibroch's music in my theme.

XXXVII

Chan e àilleachd do dhealbha,
àilleachd cruth t' aodainn,
àilleachd mo dhallabhrat
ged a dh'fhalbh i thar smaointean,
ach àilleachd an anama
bha dealbhach nad aodann,
àilleachd an spioraid,
smior cridhe mo ghaoil-sa.

XXXVII

It was not your body's beauty,
or the beauty of your brilliant face,
blaze of that blinding bandage
that dazzled my hurt eyes,
but the impeccable spirit's beauty
that moved within my haunted gaze,
the clear beauty of your spirit,
that was the marrow of my praise.

XLII

TRAIGHEAN

Nan robh sinn an Talasgar air an tràigh
far a bheil am beul mòr bàn
a' fosgladh eadar dà ghiall chruaidh,
Rubha nan Clach 's am Bioda Ruadh,
sheasainn-sa ri taobh na mara
ag ùrachadh gaoil nam anam
fhad 's a bhiodh an cuan a' lìonadh
camas Thalasgair gu sìorraidh:
sheasainn an siud air lom na tràghad
gu 'n cromadh Preiseal a cheann àigich.

Agus nan robh sinn cuideachd
air tràigh Chalgaraidh am Muile,
eadar Alba is Tiriodh,
eadar an saoghal 's a' bhiothbhuan,
dh'fhuirichinn an siud gu luan
a' tomhas gainmhich bruan air bhruain.
Agus an Uidhist air tràigh Hòmhstaidh
fa chomhair farsaingeachd na h-ònrachd,
dh'fheithinn-sa an siud gu sìorraidh,
braon air bhraon an cuan a' sìoladh.

Agus nan robh mi air tràigh Mhùideart
còmhla riut, a nodhachd ùidhe,
chuirinn suas an co-chur gaoil dhut
an cuan 's a' ghaineamh, bruan air bhraon dhiubh.
'S nan robh sinn air Mol Steinnseil Stamhain
's an fhàirge neo-aoibhneach a' tarraing
nan ulbhag is gan tilgeil tharainn,
thogainn-sa am balla daingeann
ro shìorraidheachd choimhich 's i framhach.

XLII

If we were in Talisker on the shore
where the great white foaming mouth of water
opens between two jaws as hard as flint -
the Headland of Stones and the Red Point -
I'd stand forever by the waves
renewing love out of their crumpling graves
as long as the sea would be going over
the Bay of Talisker forever;
I would stand there by the filling tide
till Preshal bowed his stallion head.

And if the two of us were together
on the shores of Calgary in Mull
between Scotland and Tiree,
between this world and eternity,
I'd stand there till time was done
counting the sands grain by grain.
And also on Uist, on Hosta's shore,
in the face of solitude's fierce stare,
I'd remain standing, without sleep,
while sea were ebbing, drop by drop.

And if I were on Moidart's shore
with you, my novelty of desire,
I'd offer this synthesis of love,
grain and water, sand and wave.
And were we by the shelves of Staffin
where the huge joyless sea is coughing
stones and boulders from its throat,
I'd build a fortified wall
against eternity's savage howl.

XLIII

Mur b' e thusa bhiodh an Cuilithionn
na mhùr eagarra gorm
a' crioslachadh le bhalla-crìche
na tha nam chridhe borb.

Mur b' e thusa bhiodh a' ghaineamh
tha 'n Talasgar dùmhail geal
na clàr biothbhuan do mo dhùilean,
air nach tilleadh an rùn-ghath.

'S mur b' e thusa bhiodh na cuantan
nan luasgan is nan tàmh
a' togail càir mo bhuadhan,
ga cur air suaimhneas àrd.

'S bhiodh am monadh donn riabhach
agus mo chiall co-shìnt' -
ach chuir thusa orra riaghladh
os cionn mo phianaidh fhìn.

Agus air creachainn chèin fhàsmhor
chinn blàthmhor craobh nan teud,
na meangach duillich t' aodann,
mo chiall is aogas rèil.

XLIII

If it weren't for you, the Cuillin
would be a level wall of blue
encircling with its tight belt
my heart's barbarous retinue.

If it weren't for you, the numerous sand
that lies on Talisker's compact shore
would be the tablet of my wishes
without the sting of salt desire.

If it weren't for you, the huge seas
both in their motion and their rest
would raise the sea-foam of my mind
to a monument on a calm coast.

While the flat, brown and brindled moorland
and my clear intellect would be
drowsing together if it weren't
for the sovereign force of your decree.

And on the distant barren rock
there grew the harp of blossomed fire
and in its branches was your face,
my reason, semblance of a star.

XLV

Rinn sgian m' eanchainn gearradh
air cloich mo ghaoil, a luaidh,
is sgrùd a faobhar gach aon bhearradh
is ghabh mo shùil a thuar.

Thionndaidh mi gach mìrean lèige
fon ghlainne gheur fhuair
a tha nam lasair cèille
a dh'fheuch iad ceudan uair.

An dèis sgine, glainne, teine
is gath nam faobhar giar,
beumadh, gearradh, losgadh, sgrùdadh,
cha robh caochladh air a fiamh.

An t-sian-chlach geàrrt' am mìle mìrean
cho slàn 's a bha i riamh,
air a prannadh ann am fùdar
ach dùmhail leugach giar.

Mar a rachadh i an àireamh
nam bruan geàrrte prann
's ann a ghabhadh i aonachd
na h-aonar cruaidh teann.

Dh'at i gu meud mìle chuantan
is chaidh gach bruan na bhraon,
ach b' i uisge chaidh an cruadal
le teannachadh at gaoil.

Bha a' chlach a fhuair a gearradh
às m' aigne chumhang fhìn
air a bearradh gus a' mhòrachd
a thoilleadh domhain-thìr.

XLV

The knife of my intellect made a cut
in my love's stubborn stone.
The blade tested every part.
Its scrutiny was keen.

I turned each section of the stone
to the inspecting glass
of the intellect sparkling in its own
chill and searching space.

But after glass and knife and fire
and the blade's piercing ray,
after the cutting, burning stare,
there was no change in the stone's hue.

The enchanted stone cut by the ardour
of my keen intelligence
(though pounded lightly into powder)
remained entire and hard and dense.

And the more it was broken to a myriad
scattered pieces in my sight
the more it became a monad,
compact, adamant and white.

It expanded to a thousand oceans,
each part a drop within a wave,
But all the water in its motion
contracted to my massive love.

The stone my intellect had cut
in its cold hard inspecting course
gathered to the arrogant light
and majesty of a universe.

Pioct' às mo chom, bha a meudachd
os cionn mo thomhais chèin
's mar bhruan chrùb a creag-màthar
am Betelgeuse nan reul.

A' chlach ghaoil a thàinig à m' eanchainn
's i ghabh am meanmna treun
gu robh i na màthair-meanmna
d' a màthair-eanchainn fhèin.

'S e 'n gaol ginte leis a' chridhe
an gaol tha 'n geimhlich shaoir
an uair a ghabhas e na spiorad
gaol eanchainn air a ghaol.

Agus 's e a' chlach tha briste
an leug shoilleir shlàn
nuair phrannar i le eanchainn
gu barrachd cruais a gràidh.

A luaidh, mur biodh gaol mo chridhe
ort mar chruas na lèig,
tha fhios gun gabhadh e gearradh
le eanchainn chruaidh gheur.

Struck from my breast, its greatness
was measureless to my eye.
It crouched in its giant brightness
like Betelgeuse in the sky.

The love-stone springing from my head
by paradox of active passion
became the genesis of the red
skies of the mind's imagination.

The love begotten by the heart
is a love that dances in its chains
when it embraces intellect—
love of the scrutinising brain.

And the stone that's always broken
by the assiduous mind
becomes a bright entire stone
made harder by each new wound.

Dearest, if my heart's love
were not as strong as the jewelled stone,
surely the intellectual knife
would have cut it from my flesh and bone.

XLVIII

Mar riutsa tha m' irisleachd
co-ionann rim uaill
agus tha m' ùmhlachd is m' àrdan
nan ceòl-gàire buan.

Sleuchdt' aig do chasan tha mo spiorad
air chorra-bhioda àrd
agus tha pian is luasgan m' aigne
nam bras shuaimhneas tàimh.

'S nad fhaisge tha a' chòmhail
a th' agam rium fhèin
cho dlùth rium ri smior mo chridhe
's e falbh air binnean cèin.

Fhuair mi faoisgneadh às a' chochall
a rinn cor mo rèis
is dhiùchd barr-guc m' anama
bho arraban na lèig.

XLVIII

With you my humility
is equal to my pride:
my arrogance and obedience
on one great music-ride.

Stretched at your feet my tall spirit
on high tip-toe goes,
my pain and restlessness assume
a headlong repose.

And beside you the dialogue
I hold with myself each hour
is near me as my heart's marrow
moving on mountains far.

I've been unhusked from the dead husk
which once sealed me round.
A perfect summer of new birth
steps from the sorrow of my mind.

XLIX

Bha 'm bàt' agam fo sheòl 's a' Chlàrach
a' gàireachdaich fo sròin,
mo làmh cheàrr air falmadair
's an tèile 'n suaineadh sgòid.

Air dara tobhta 'n fhuaraidh
shuidh thu, luaidh, nam chòir
agus do ròp laist cuailein
mum chrìdh na shuaineadh òir.

A Dhia, nan robh an cùrsa ud
gu mo cheann-uidhe deòin,
cha bhiodh am Buta Leòdhasach
air fòghnadh do mo sheòl.

XLIX

My boat was sailing on the Clàrach
in a benign and ocean smile,
my right hand was on the tiller,
my left in the winding of the sail.

On the second thwart to windward
you sat, my youthful dear,
my swelling heart entangled
in the ropes of your lighted hair.

God, if that course were steady
to the harbour of my will,
not even the Butt of Lewis
would appease my thirsty sail.

L

Chan eil anns a' bhròn ach neoini
's chan eil anns a' ghaol ach bruan
fa chomhair nan reul a' sgaoileadh
's an saoghal a' dol na chuairt.

Agus liuthad millean bliadhna
on thriall an Talamh na chaoir
agus liuthad millean iadhadh
a thug e le thriall air gaol.

Dè dhòmhsa a mhillean iadhadh,
dè dhòmhsa a chian chùrs' aost
a chionn nach toir e le ghrian leus
gnè shìorraidheachd do mo ghaol?

Seatadh e fad rèis a bhuantachd
tro chluaintean glasa nan speur
a chionn nach dealbhar le buaidh e
na chumadh luaidhe dom chèill!

A chionn nach eil suim dar miannan
anns an iadhadh bhiothbhuan chlaon
chan eil mo shuim-sa r' a cheudan
no mhilleanan sgeulachd gaoil.

Nam b' urrainn aodann mo luaidhe
bhith àlainn is buan gu bràth
bheirinn dùbhlan do Thìm le bhuadhan,
le nodhachd 's le luathghair fàis.

L

Grief is scaled to zero and
love itself of little price
beneath the spread of the great stars
and earth revolving in space.

And the many many million years
since the earth's core blazed red-hot.
And the many many million twists
its irony has given love's plot.

What to me its twistings
and what to me its ancient grave
illustrious circuit, since its sun
will not immortalise my love?

Let its great journeys be endless
through the grey plains of the skies
since it is powerless to shape
what my bare intellect can prize.

Since it's indifferent to our wishes,
its slanting course repetitive,
why should I heed its hundred fictions,
the million stories of its love?

If the beautiful face of my darling
would be always beautiful to my gaze
I would astonish time itself
with the inventive novelties of my praise.

LII

Dom dhùr-amharc bha thu nad reul
's tu leat fhèin san iarmailt:
is thugadh dhut an dà leus
lem aigne thorrach 's m' iargain.

'S an uair sin bhoillsg thu le trì
an aon leus dìreach trianaid:
ach cha robh nam leòis dhian fhìn
ach clann do lìthe 'n iargain.

Bha mi feitheamh ris a' bheum
a mhilleadh do rèim le chrìonadh;
ach thug mi dhut na trì dhut fhèin
an ceann rèis deich bliadhna.

Oir nam b' iad mo leòis gin fhìn
a bheòthaich lì nad lias-sa,
bu chinnt gun cailleadh iad am brìgh
le glasadh tìm deich bliadhna.

A shuilbhireachd 's a chridhe chòir
's sibh lòghmhor ann an aodann:
a mheallaidh cridhe 's a mheallaidh sùla,
ur n-ìomhaigh rùin a h-aogas!

Cha b' ann fada bha an tòir
a thug còrr 's deich bliadhna
an uair a bha an fhaodail còrr
's na dh'fhògnadh dòchas sìorraidh.

LII

To my scrutiny you were a star
shining in the sky's roof
and you were given the two lights
of my fertile spirit and my grief.

And therefore you blazed with three,
in one trinity, fire-bright.
But these, my vehement lights, were only
echoes of your own light.

I waited for the power that would
disfigure your virtue in its course:
but I offered you the three together
at the end of ten years.

Though if it were my own two lights
that gave such splendid power to yours
surely their brightness would be quenched
by brutal time in ten years.

O cheerfulness and open heart
ablaze in a clear virtuous face:
deceit of heart, deceit of eyes
so imaged in your lustrous grace.

Surely not long was that pursuit
though it was ten years and more—
when a chance sight of beauty brought
the hope an eternity could desire.

LIV

Bu tu camhanaich air a' Chuilithionn
's latha suilbhir air a' Chlàraich,
grian air a h-uilinn anns an òr-shruth
agus ròs geal bristeadh fàire.

Lainnir sheòl air linne ghrianaich,
gorm a' chuain is iarmailt àr-bhuidh,
an òg-mhadainn na do chuailean
's na do ghruaidhean soilleir àlainn.

Mo leug camhanaich is oidhche
t' aodann 's do choibhneas gràdhach,
ged tha bior glas an dòlais
tro chliabh m' òg-mhaidne sàthte.

LIV

You were a daybreak on the Cuilithionn,
a happy light across the Clàrach,
sun on her elbow in the gold-stream
and the candid rose of dawning.

Glitter of sails on sunny waters,
blue of sea and hue of harvest,
burning in your golden tresses
and in your cheeks as bright as morning.

Jewel of my dawn and night-time,
countenance of lovely kindness,
though the bitter shaft of mourning
in your dawning breast is shining.

LV

Chan fhaic mi fàth mo shaothrach
bhith cur smaointean an cainnt bhàsmhoir,
a-nis is siùrsachd na Roinn-Eòrpa
na murt stòite 's na cràdhlot;
ach thugadh dhuinn am milleann bliadhna
na mhìr an roinn chianail fhàsmhoir,
gaisge 's foighidinn nan ceudan
agus mìorbhail aodainn àlainn.

LV

I cannot see the sense
of writing in a dying tongue
now that Europe, raped and torn,
moans behind my song.
But we were given a million years,
from sorrowful time a bitter slice,
the patience and courage of the many,
the miracle of a lovely face.

LVI

Na mo dheich bliadhna saothrach
riamh cha d' fhuair mi dàn air faodail
cho suaimhneach ri do chuailean craobhach,
cho àlainn fosgailte ri t' aodann.

LVI

In my ten years of striving
never once did I compose
a song as calm as your branching tresses,
as lovely and open as your face.

'Tha e labhairt ri mo chridhe
nach fhaodar sgaradh a shireadh
eadar miann agus susbaint
a' chuspair dho-ruighinn'

LVII

Tha aodann ga mo thathaich,
ga mo leantainn dh'oidhche 's latha:
tha aodann buadhmhor nìghne
's e sìor agairt.

Tha e labhairt ri mo chridhe
nach fhaodar sgaradh a shireadh
eadar miann agus susbaint
a' chuspair dho-ruighinn,

nach tig tubaist air àilleachd
a dh'aindeoin cinntinn nam fàiling
a chionn gu bheil là aomte
cho saor ri là màireach,

agus gu bheil an tràth seo
os cionn gach caochlaidh 's àichidh
a ni ceannairc èigheach
ra rèim a-màireach,

a chionn gu bheil i 'n dràsta
gum bi 'cruth 's a bith gu bràth ann
agus nach urrainn caochladh
a h-aonachd a mhàbadh,

gu bheil roghainn miann na sùla
cho biothbhuan ris na rùintean
a ghabh an cumadh sìorraidh
am briathran ùra,

LVII

I'm haunted by a face
that pursues me night and day,
the marvellous face of my darling
with its eternal cry.

It's always speaking to my heart
that even time will never part
its gifted substance from desire -
implacable theme of my prayer:

that she will never lose uniqueness
though assailed by every human weakness
and that a yesterday is as free
as spacious tomorrow will be:

and that the present time's above
alteration in our love,
and tomorrow's no fierce rebel to
the sovereign acres we renew:

and that the future will allow
changeless eternity to her Now,
now will such brilliance be flawed
by time's thievery and fraud:

that bodies by desire's force
can be as permanent as the verse
which that desire itself made
from vivid substance, not from shade:

gu bheil i cheart cho àghmhor
ri ealain an dà Phàdraig
ged nach cuir an cèill i
ceòl rèidh no clach gheàrrte,

's ged nach fhaod clàr dealbha
a cruth 's a dreach a thairgsinn
do na gineil ùra
gun smùradh coirbte.

O aodainn, aodainn, aodainn,
an caill, an caill thu 'n t-ioghnadh
leis na ghlac do bhòidhche
sòlas faoilidh?

Mur gabh clach no clàr do shamhladh
dè ni ealaidh chiùil no ranntachd
mur eil seòl an tràth seo
chur an càs staimhnte,

mur eil seòl air bacadh
na h-uarach seo 's a glacadh
an gainmhich a' chaochlaidh
le faobhar acrach,

mun tog i na siùil ùra
gu dìochuimhne air chùrsa
's mun caillear a brèidean
bho lèirsinn sùla?

O aodainn a tha gam thathaich,
aodainn àlainn a tha labhairt,
an triall thu leis an àm seo
neo-ar-thaing t' agairt?

that, untransmuted into paint,
her beauty still is eloquent,
for how could portraiture transmit
the Venus of her sparkling wit,

without untruthfulness to those
who study what our hands compose?

O marvellous miraculous face,
will you ever lose that grace
you caught by a rare chance from this
hurricane through which we pass?

If neither paint nor sculpture can
truthfully master what you mean,
how can my wandering music fix
your face above the idiot Styx

if there's no way to wind our time
into a solid diagram
or there's no way to shape this present
into the metaphor we fashioned,

if there's no way to save our ship
with the hooked anchor's grappling grip
before her swelling sails go down
into the ocean of her ruin,

before her equipage is quite
lost to the tears of our sight.

O face that always haunts me,
face that is always speaking,
will you companion dying time
in spite of your weeping?

Nuair chrìonas tasgadh gach cuimhne
a bheir gaol no smuain no suim dhut,
an caill thu mealladh t' aonachd
's tu faoin gun chuimhn' ort?

Chan iarrainn-sa gu bràth dhut
aon bhiothbhuantachd dod àilleachd
ach na liùbhradh slàn i
dìreach mar a tha i.

Chan iarrainn gnìomhachd a' chiùil
's e ioma-bhriathrach ri ùidh:
chan iarrainn aon nì ùr
nach fhaca mi fhìn nad ghnùis.

Agus cha tugadh clàr dathte
do chuimhne ach aon aiteal
ged chuimteadh trian ded bhuadhan
na thuar an tasgadh.

Mar sin, a thràth is aodainn,
feumar ur cuideachd daonnan
los nach bi 'n ceann na h-uarach
buadhan aomte.

A thràth de thìm nuair dh'fhalbhas
do rèim mar an allacheò,
dè am breannachadh ùr-laist'
don diùchd t' fhalbhan?

O thràth de thìm, 's na thrèigeas
dhinne le do cheuman,
càit a bheil an cùrsa
bheir ùidh dhuinn no sgeul oirnn?

When every mind in which you were
withers along its wintry air,
is your diminished beauty wrecked
with memory and intellect?

But I would never ask for you
any eternity but this -
your beauty as it now is,
this permanence and none but this.

Nor would the intricate song suffice
to stand impeccable in your place
nor would I ask for a novel grace
to be added to your loved face.

And a painted picture would be
mere shadow of your memory
though a third part of what you were
by miracle should blossom there.

Therefore your face and time must be
together in eternity
in order that time itself will not
decline with you into night.

O present time when you are past
like the windings of a troubled mist,
into what meaning do you pour
every minute, every hour?

O present time when part of us
dies along your ominous course,
how should we steer our ship to find
a true meaning for the mind?

Na bha, 's na tha an dràsta,
ged mhaireadh iad gu bràth dhinn,
ciamar thigeadh sgeul orr'
bho chèin-thràighean?

Dè 'n t-sùil a nì am faicinn
no chluas a nì an claisteachd
's iad air turas faondraidh
bhàrr smaointean aigne?

Ciod e an ceathramh seòl-tomhais
a bheir an àilleachd seo fa chomhair
sùla, reusain no aon chàileachd
thar fàsaichean glomhair?

Is dè a' chàil thar chàiltean
a mhothaicheas an àilleachd,
nuair nach nochd sùil no cluas i,
blas, suathadh no fàileadh,

's nuair nach bi i paisgte
an cuimhne bheò no 'm faisge
ris na smuainteanan siùbhlach
a dh'ùraicheas an tasgadh?

Mur faighear, air chor 's gum mothaich,
aon chàil eile no seòl-tomhais,
am bi cruth no bith aig t' àilleachd
an àrainn tìme 's domhainn?

O aodainn a tha gam thathaich,
O mhìorbhail a tha labhar,
a bheil aon phort an tìm dhut
no balla-crìch ach talamh?

And though the present and the past
were to stand solid as a post,
where would it point to? From what land
would blow a truth we'd understand?

How could we truly hear or see
what their significance could be
who take their devious senseless course
past our magnetic fields of force?

What fourth dimension can bring
such beauty into the naked ring
of eye, reason, sense or taste
past chasms of the deathly waste?

What abstract Sense above all sense
will notice beauty's eloquence
when sight, hearing, touch and taste
and smell itself will have gone waste?

And when that beauty isn't locked
in memory or intellect
but is distant from the lively mind
renewing what its thought designed?

And if neither of these, by true invention—
a sixth sense or fourth dimension—
will keep beauty in clear sight,
must time glut its appetite?

O face that always haunts me,
eloquent miracle of light,
will earth be your only harbour
and the dense clay your night?

O luathghair dhaonda chuimir,
a bheil seòl-tomhais sa chruinne
a bheir dhut barrachd slànachd
na ceòl no clàr no luinneag?

Ma tha Arm Dearg a' chinne
an gleac bàis ri taobh an Dniepeir,
chan e euchd a ghaisge
as fhaisg' air mo chridhe,

ach aodann a tha gam thathaich,
ga mo leantainn dh'oidhche 's latha,
aodann buadhmhor nìghne
's e sìor labhairt.

O marvellous and exultant joy,
is there no way to keep you strong
except by portraiture or music
or my imperfect devious song?

And if the Red Army is fighting
for its life along the Dnieper River,
it's not its heroic exploits
that now arouse my fever

but a face that always haunts me,
that pursues me night and day,
the marvellous face of my darling
with its eternal cry.